CAIRNS

REEF TO RAINFOREST

D1366162

Photography by Peter Jarver
Master of Photography, AIPP

Text by Robert Reid

Other books by Peter Jarver:

The Top End of Down Under
Kakadu Country
The Heart of Australia
Darwin, Australia's Northern Capital

Cairns ~ Jewel of the North

Cairns is a bustling city on the move, rapidly overtaking larger centres in southern states and other parts of Queensland as the tourist city of the future. Once viewed as a sleepy tropical outpost "up north", Cairns has emerged in the past ten years as a confident challenger for the title of Australia's fastest growing city.

Already it is ranked fourth, boosted by a rapidly increasing influx of tourists attracted to its easy-going lifestyle and diversity of environment. There are few places in the world that can offer its visitors natural wonders such as the Great Barrier Reef, pristine World Heritage rainforest, coastal wetlands and the rolling hills of the Atherton Tableland - all on the city's doorstep. Cairns is in a positive mood, opening up a northern gateway to Australia's Asian neighbours and the rest of the world. The city has a sense of destiny and purpose as it moves towards the twenty-first century.

But it wasn't always like this. Cairns had its beginnings in a pioneering saga of mud, toil and everyday heroism that was a trademark of north Queensland's early settlers.

One hundred and six years after Captain James Cook named Trinity Bay during his journey northwards through the treacherous waters of the Barrier Reef, a small party of men struggled ashore to establish a campsite that was to become the city of Cairns. It was October 6, 1876, and the party had sailed from Townsville on board the "Porpoise" with the express intention of opening up a port for the collection of custom duties. It was tough going. The men had to hack their way through dense mangroves to set up tents on a strip of sand. The area surrounding them was an inhospitable wilderness of swamps, thick scrub, brackish lagoons and sandbars. Prior to their arrival, the area had been used by Aborigines and occasional beche-de-mer fishermen. It was only the recent discovery of gold in the Cape York hinterland that prompted an official settlement of the site.

Cairns was named after the Governor of Queensland, Sir William Wellington Cairns, the next day, October 7, on what must have been a dismal occasion in the mosquito-infested scrub. On November 1, Trinity Bay was declared a port of entry, and Cairns opened its first official building - the Post Office - which consisted of an empty brandy case hung on a tent pole!

That same year, gold prospector William Smith established a rival settlement on the banks of the Barron River, near present-day Smithfield. It rapidly became a brawling, rollicking shanty town frequented by packers and miners - and by sharp-eyed businessmen who saw potential in this new rival to the port of Cairns. For a short time the future of Cairns was threatened by Smithfield's success but a devastating cyclone in 1877 solved the coastal settlement's problem. Smithfield was destroyed by flood and never rebuilt.

But Cairns' troubles were far from over. The

destruction of Smithfield saw the emergence of Port Douglas as an alternative port, and the gold trade gradually drifted to the north. Over the next few years, Cairns went into an economic slump, and many thought the town was doomed. As proof of this, the government moved the District Court and the Land Office to Port Douglas. Commerce in the fledgling town almost came to a halt - only the cedar cutters working in the nearby ranges kept the town alive.

Against the odds, Cairns survived its early setbacks, and when tin was discovered at Herberton and Irvinebank, the town once again forged ahead. By the end of 1882 sugar cane plantations were established and talk of a rail link to the Atherton Tableland created great excitement among traders in the area. Government surveyors were sent into the field to investigate possible routes and in April 1884 the Barron valley was announced as the preferred option. Cairns' bitter rival, Port Douglas, suffered a major economic blow as a result of the decision. Cairns had won its long fight for survival. In 1886, construction began on the now famous Kuranda railway line.

But if any one thing was responsible for the survival and success of Cairns it was the sugar industry. One of the first sugar growing pioneers, Andrew Lee On, was responsible for the construction of the first crushing mill in 1881. A year later, more than 100,000 acres had been selected around Cairns to grow sugar. The golden age of sugar cane in north Queensland had begun.

Cairns' population was boosted by the arrival of Chinese from the goldfields. They grew crops of bananas, rice, pineapples and citrus fruits. The enterprising Chinese were responsible for the establishment of three rice mills in 1889 and at one stage were exporting 500,000 bunches of bananas a year.

In May 1885, Cairns was proclaimed a municipality and the first mayor, Richard Ash Kingsford, took office. Mayor Kingsford's grandson, Charles Kingsford Smith, was later to become the world's most celebrated aviator. In 1903, Cairns was proclaimed a town, and by 1923 a city, with a population of 20,000 citizens.

Despite its prosperity and status as a town, Cairns at the turn of the century was still a rough and tumble outpost built primarily on a series of sandbars running parallel to the foreshore. For years, mud and sand were carted - often by wheelbarrow - from the beach and mangroves and dumped in gullies and swamps. Gradually, streets and buildings took the place of areas once traversed by planks and an occasional footbridge. Buildings on the waterfront were constructed on pylons to keep them above high tides and wet season floods.

Heat, rain and mud were realities of life in the early days of Cairns. It took nine years for the town to be cleared and surveyed. The town survived into the twentieth century because of the pioneering spirit of its founders, the men and women who rejected defeat and laid the foundations for the present modern, sophisticated city of Cairns.

Above: Rays of sunlight sweep across the coastal plains of Cairns, highlighting Trinity Inlet and Cape Grafton.

Cairns ~ City of the Future

Sugar is as vital to north Queensland today as it was one hundred years ago. Together with tourism, the familiar swaying fields of cane around Cairns symbolise the solid heart of the region's economic strength. Throughout its colourful history, Cairns has always been linked to sugar. Even though valuable cane land is under siege from developers, the importance of sugar crops seems likely to continue.

The area's six mills crush approximately six million tonnes of cane annually, yielding an estimated gross financial return of $314 million into north Queensland's economy. Sugar growing in recent years has spread to the Atherton Tableland, notably around Mareeba, where it is expected to replace tobacco as the primary crop. An extra crushing mill on the Tableland is planned for the future as the industry expands in that region.

Tropical fruit production also contributes to the wealth of north Queensland, with banana crops growing at the rate of 15 percent every year for the past decade. Bananas add a further $154 million annually to the economy. Pawpaws, lychees, mangoes and a wide variety of rare and exotic fruits have combined to make Cairns the hub of the nation's "fruit basket".

Mining, the industry that gave birth to the city, is still a traditional mainstay of the region's success and has reached a current $400 million earning capacity.

Cairns' boom industry, however, is the movement of people. Tourism during the past decade has transformed the city into a cosmopolitan crossroads for international travellers and Australian holiday-makers. Cairns is now a mecca for budget-conscious back-packers, millionaire jet-setters and shrewd investors keen to become part of the region's success. The city has lifted its image to become the success story of Australian tourism in the Nineties, turning over $900 million in revenue every year.

Ranked number 21 in 1976, Cairns is now the 16th largest city in Australia. The city has doubled its population since 1971 and is expected to reach 120,000 in its greater area by 1996. Cairns airport is the nation's sixth busiest, handling traffic from seven international airlines and two domestic carriers, while the Port of Cairns, about to undergo a major reconstruction, is Australia's second busiest port of call for luxury cruise ships.

The city heart is about to be transformed with a casino, convention centre and a giant retail complex to be completed over the next five years. For a city 1500km away from its big sister, Brisbane, Cairns is showing unprecedented growth and vision for the future.

Cairns is ideally situated as a base for its surrounding

attractions. The northern highway follows a string of spectacular, unspoiled beaches until it reaches Cairns' old rival, Port Douglas, now a modern beach resort, just south of the sugar town of Mossman. From there, the Daintree River and Cape Tribulation share the boundaries of magnificent wet tropics rainforest.

West from Cairns the Atherton Tableland is a cool plateau of volcanic lakes, rolling pasture lands, waterfalls and historic buildings. Further west, Chillagoe presents a stark contrast to the coastal and Tableland landscapes. Limestone bluffs sculpted by nature stand guard over cave systems that burrow deep below their jagged exteriors. Chillagoe, once a mining town, is now famous as the site of recently discovered marble deposits, reputed to be the finest in the world.

Above all, Cairns sits on the water's edge of the Great Barrier Reef, a natural starting point for visits to one of the truly great wonders of the world. Visitors choose trips to coral cays, tropical islands, reefs and white-sand beaches, or longer cruises north to Lizard Island and other destinations on the Reef. Whatever the choice, it can be arranged in Cairns, a city where literally thousands of travel plans are organised every day.

Internationally recognised as a world leader in developing ways of presenting reefs to the public, the city is home to a select group of innovators who pioneered research into underwater observatories, semi-submersible viewing craft and the high-tech super-catamaran vessels now exported to overseas markets.

Cairns is a tolerant city, proud of its many ethnic groups that help make north Queensland the diverse and interesting place it is. It is conscious of its new-found destiny - that of a robust, dynamic meeting place of cultures, ideas and events. There is a strong Asian influence in the city and business leaders hold a growing belief that Cairns will become an important administrative link between southern capitals and the blossoming trade centres of the Asia-Pacific region. Tokyo, Singapore and Hong Kong are a mere six hours flying time from Cairns - no distance at all for today's business elite. After all, Japanese executives already jet into Cairns for a game of golf!

In this northern city of the future, Taiwanese businessmen rub shoulders with German back-packers and American tourists share their reef trips with Japanese honeymooners and Australian families. Crowded nightclubs show a multicultural kaleidoscope of faces. Street scenes abound with signs in different languages. Cairns, founded less than a hundred and twenty years ago in the mud and dense mangrove swamps of Trinity Bay, has emerged as a bright star on Australia's northern horizon.

Above: Twilight reveals the long sweep of the Northern Beaches, Cairns city visible in the distance.

Trinity Inlet and Marlin Marina provide a safe haven for both commercial boats and cruising yachts.

The view across Trinity Inlet and the Pier towards Cairns city.

A fiery sunset glows late into this evening view of Cairns city.

Looking north along the Esplanade at dusk.

The distinctive domed roof of the Reef Hotel Casino is a new addition to Cairns' changing waterfront precinct.

Built as government offices in 1936, the Cairns Regional Gallery is now the main focal point for the city's artistic endeavours.

Boland's Centre opened as Cairns' original department store in 1914.

This fine example of a Queenslander-style house was built in 1939.

Rainforested lobby of the Radisson Plaza Hotel.

The Pier shopping complex.

With crowds of locals and tourists , Rusty's Market is a bustle of activity and a feast of colour.

A sailing ship from a bygone era returns to Cairns after a leisurely day exploring the reef.

Trinity Wharf bustles with activity as tourists set out for the reef on one of the fast new catamarans.

The Mangrove Boardwalk near Cairns Airport is remarkable for both the size and diversity of mangrove species found there.

Pink Lotus lilies are a feature of the Centenary Lakes near the Flecker Botanic Gardens.

The Rainforest Boardwalk opposite the Botanic Gardens passes through a natural swamp rainforest dominated by Alexander palms.

Yachts moored in Trinity Inlet with Walsh's Pyramid in the background.

A busy morning in Trinity Inlet with tourist boats weaving a passage through starters in a yacht race.

Flagstaff Hill in Port Douglas affords an excellent view onto one of the year's main yachting races.

Snorkellers explore the shallow waters of Moore Reef.

KURANDA SCENIC RAILWAY

Riding the Kuranda Scenic Railway for the first time, it becomes immediately apparent to the visitor why it is regarded as one of the great train journeys of the world. Snaking its way 34 kilometres up the contours of a mountain range, the train passes through 15 tunnels, and crosses Stoney Creek Bridge, before stopping at Barron Falls and ending its journey at picturesque Kuranda Railway Station, 328 metres above the city of Cairns.

Along the way, train travellers gaze out across coastal valleys, spectacular Barron Gorge and the sparkling blue waters of the Great Barrier Reef. Visitors to Cairns are quick to realise the view from the train can't be matched by road, and every trip is a photographer's delight. The leisurely ninety minute journey allows time to enjoy the mountain environment and reflect on the colourful history of the railway line's construction. It's a story of an engineering feat that pays tribute to the men who waged a five year battle against the elements to make a dream come true.

On May 10, 1886 Cairns celebrated the beginning of the railway when the Premier of Queensland, Samuel Griffith, symbolically turned the first spade-full of earth - reputedly with a silver spade! It was an important occasion for the fledgling town and boisterous celebrations continued on throughout the night.

The first section of Cairns' new railway ran 13 kilometres to Redlynch and took 18 months to build. It was a difficult task, as the line had to traverse the usual mangrove swamplands and mudflats that were typical of the area. Mosquitoes and sandflies made life on the line unpleasant and dangerous. Men died of what was simply called "coastal fever" - probably scrub typhus and malaria. Snakes and ticks abounded in the swamps and bite victims usually died. These early fatalities set the stage for a construction epic that would cost many human lives.

The range section of the railway was awarded to contractor John Robb, a highly respected engineer who had built bridges in southern states with great success. Robb set up his construction headquarters on the Barron River near present day Kamerunga, established a sawmill and quarries, and carefully planned his assault on the formidable mountain range.

It was to be an engineering feat with few equals of the day. From April 1887, when he started work on the range section, until its completion in June 1891, Robb had to overcome the considerable problems of constructing 15 tunnels, more than two kilometres of bridgework, and negotiate 98 bends - some of them solid rock that had to be broken down by men suspended from ropes before rail benches could be formed.

At one time, over 1000 men were at work on the project, some of them living with wives and children in campsite "towns" along the route. It was an international workforce, many of them Irish labourers and Italians recruited specifically for the job. Life in the camps was a wild, noisy affair, with all night alcoholic sessions commonplace. One enterprising Cairns businessman, Michael Boland, built a substantial hotel at Camp Oven Creek, near No. 15 Tunnel - one of the larger camps. Boland later established a department store in Cairns and the building has been preserved as part of the city's historic heritage. No. 15 Tunnel was the site of a tragedy in April 1889 when seven men died in a cave-in just inside the entrance. It was the railway's last tunnel, but also the most dangerous. Work was held up for eight months while the accident was investigated.

Nobody knows how many men died on the mountainside. About 30 fatalities were recorded, but foreign navvies often lost their lives without official recognition. Rock falls and collapsing tunnels were common and unstable blasting powder was known to have killed unlucky handlers. It was a project fraught with danger and the men knew it. They faced each new day with death looking over their shoulder, but, in the spirit of the times, they got on with the job at hand with few complaints.

On March 12, 1891, the first ballast train reached Barron Falls and a month later, Kuranda. On June 25, the first passengers arrived in the rainforest township. John Robb held a luncheon at Barron Falls to mark the occasion. Robb left the north after his remarkable achievement, leaving behind a railway that would become world famous for its breathtaking scenery. Robb's Monument, a huge stone boulder overlooking the rail at the top of the range, stands in honour of the man who completed one of the most difficult tasks of his time.

Above: The Kuranda train passes over the bridge at Stoney Creek Falls.

Travellers on the Kuranda Scenic Railway gain an excellent view of Barron Falls in flood.

An early morning fog cloaks the Kuranda Railway Station and Skyrail terminal.

Kuranda Markets

Kuranda, the world famous "Village in the Rainforest", was for many years a sleepy town nestling quietly in the Macalister Range overlooking Cairns.

A handful of shops and two hotels catered to the locals and weekend visitors from Cairns who caught the train or drove up the range to escape the coastal heat.

The town was jokingly referred to as the "air-conditioned suburb" of Cairns and seemed destined to remain a quaint holiday retreat for city dwellers.

But all that changed in the late Sixties when Kuranda was discovered by hippies from the south who invaded the town and changed its character forever. With land at throwaway prices, the new-age settlers established communes and created an alternative lifestyle image for the town - an image that attracted attention. Curious visitors began to arrive, eager for a glimpse of naked hippie bathers frolicking in the Barron River and strolling the main street in their bizarre clothing. Although Kuranda residents didn't realise it at the time, a new industry had been born - tourism.

Over the next decade, Kuranda became the home for a diverse population of artists, musicians, craftspeople, and a growing exodus of Cairns residents willing to commute daily to work in exchange for the peace and quiet of life in the hills.

Then, in mid-1978, a curious thing happened. A group of businessmen met to discuss ways of improving the town's economy and a craft market was suggested. Jim Mealing, owner of the already famous Honey House, made a block of land below his shop available, and the first Kuranda market opened on Sunday August 8 with a total of 15 stallholders. As a result of a successful advertising campaign the day was a resounding success, with both hotels and the local service station running out of food!

In early 1984 Wednesday markets were introduced in an effort to boost midweek trade in the town.

After a slow start, this too became successful, and the Kuranda business community realised the market concept was crucial to the town's economic future.

While the townspeople had paid for their own tourist train for the previous two years, Queensland Rail responded to the market's success by introducing new timetables and taking over the service completely.

Today, three trains climb the range daily, usually packed with tourists intent on three objectives - to view Barron Falls, have lunch in the town itself, and visit Kuranda Markets. Now approximately half a million people ride the scenic train from Cairns to Kuranda annually.

On the most popular market day, Sunday, an average of 135 stalls sell local craft, bric-a-brac, fruit and vegetables, clothing and take-away food. A crowd of 5,000 people, comprising an estimated 60% international visitors, browse among the stalls, shopping and making use of a foreign currency exchange service.

Even though Kuranda is a dedicated tourist town, and the streets are crowded every day with strangers, the Village in the Rainforest has managed to retain its special qualities of calmness and harmony with nature.

With a rare clarity of foresight, the town's Chamber of Commerce has deliberately encouraged daytime tourism while restricting resort development, thus ensuring long-time residents can enjoy the "old" Kuranda when the last train departs and darkness falls.

Above: Bungy jumping at the Kuranda Markets.

A visitor sits quietly while having his portrait drawn.

Jewellery, crafts, clothes and bungy jumping are features of the Kuranda Markets.

Morning fog envelops the countryside around Barron River bridge, gateway to the Tablelands.

Enormous Banyan trees form a shaded corridor through Kuranda, a village in the rainforest.

Barron Falls in flood during the Wet Season.

On a clear day the view from a Skyrail gondola takes in a distant panorama as well as the rainforest canopy.

Low cloud envelopes the rainforest, enhancing the mood as a gondola glides through the mist.

The magnificent view over cane fields and the Mulgrave River from Walsh's Pyramid.

Early morning light reveals the mountainous backdrop of Cairns.

Admiring the Curtain Fig Tree near Yungaburra.

One thousand year old twin Kauri Pines at Lake Barrine.

The lush tropical surrounds of Millaa Millaa Falls.

The fertile rolling hills of the Atherton Tableland give rise to Queensland's highest peak, Mt Bartle Frere.

The town of Mossman is surrounded by large fields of sugar cane.

Millstream Falls near Ravenshoe, on the western edge of the Atherton Tableland.

Josephine Falls is fed by water from Mount Bartle Frere, Queensland's highest peak.

Mist swirls around the upper reaches of Tully Gorge.

The Great Barrier Reef

It's the world's largest living structure - a vast coral reef rampart that stretches a staggering 2,300 kilometres along Queensland's tropical coast from Bundaberg in the south to the tip of Cape York Peninsula. It occupies nearly 350,000 square kilometres of marine territory that encompasses 2,900 individual reefs, 300 coral cays and 618 continental islands. It is a mammoth natural phenomenon teeming with life rich in diversity and beauty. In 1981, because of its outstanding value, the Great Barrier Reef was inscribed on the World Heritage List under the UNESCO Convention concerning the protection of the World Cultural and Natural Heritage. As a result of this action the Great Barrier Reef was recognised by the international community as a natural wonder to be protected for future generations.

The Great Barrier Reef is home to some 1,500 species of fish, 242 different types of birds, 22 different whales and 400 species of coral. Add to the list turtles, sea snakes, 4,000 species of molluscs and the largest population of dugong in the world and it becomes clear why the Australian Government formed the Great Barrier Reef Marine Park Authority in 1975 to protect such an important national asset.

The natural history of the Great Barrier Reef spans 15 million years, beginning when the continent of Australia had "drifted" north to waters warm enough for corals to grow. Subsequently, during a succession of global Ice Ages, the world's sea levels rose and fell by as much as 150 metres. As a result, Australia's surrounding continental shelf was alternately submerged and left high and dry as the waters receded. Coral reefs developed with each inundation but subsequently died as they were exposed, forming dry limestone hills. Some of the corals survived, however, by migrating into deeper water on the sloping outer edge of the continental shelf. The descendants of those corals continued to form new colonies on top of the skeletons of their predecessors each time the shelf was covered. In this way, the present Great Barrier Reef was formed a mere 9,000 years ago, a comparatively recent layer of living coral on top of an ancient foundation of limestone.

Coral polyps are literally the backbone of all coral reefs. They are individual animals which can be broadly divided into two groups - hard and soft corals.

The hard, or reef-building coral polyps produce limestone skeletons and then divide to form new polyps, a process of growth and division that results in massive limestone graveyards - coral reefs. Soft corals lack the rigid limestone skeletons of their cousins but are an important part of the reef, making up almost half of the living tissue on the reef surface.

Although soft corals are animals, their body tissue contains live algae which, like green land plants, absorb energy from the sun to sustain life. This symbiotic relationship between animal and plant cells also exists in hard corals and many other marine organisms. Coral polyps feed by using tentacles armed with stinging cells to paralyse microscopic sea animals in the sea around them. Soft corals, in spite of their defenceless appearance, are in fact quite deadly - capable of killing hard corals and overgrowing them with the use of toxic chemicals called terpenes, which they release into the water. The same chemical makes the polyps unappetising to predators, except for the "egg cowrie" mollusc that neutralises the poison in its own body, and that most notorious of all coral eaters, the crown of thorns starfish.

The Great Barrier Reef's most sensational show is without doubt the annual coral spawning event when, just after a full moon in late spring or early summer, corals perform a synchronised spawning "festival" that attracts world-wide attention. During a several-day period of intense activity, polyps release spherical bundles often containing hundreds of both male and female sex cells. These egg-and-sperm containers, released in their millions, float to the surface in a majestic spectacle that has been described as an underwater fireworks display and an upside down snowstorm.

When they reach the surface the bundles break open and fertilisation takes place. Within a few hours fertilised eggs begin to divide into embryos that eventually descend to the seabed to form new coral polyps. Thus the coral reef building cycle begins again.

True coral cay islands - as distinct from mainland-related "continental" islands - are formed entirely from broken

The boomerang shape of Moore Reef.

Elford Reef is a mixture of coral, sand and deep water.

coral and other sedimentary debris created from the host reefs beneath them. Wind and wave action over a long period of time causes deposits of this reef "rubble" to concentrate into a sandspit on the lee side of a reef. Vegetation may occur as plant seeds drift onto the cay or are carried there by seabirds. Eventually, the coral cay may become a wooded island, but will always remain unstable, changing shape as tides and tropical cyclones erode its sandy edges. Green Island, just 27km from Cairns, is a typical coral cay island. Two thirds of the 12 hectare island is national park and its close proximity to a major city has made it the most visited coral cay on the Great Barrier Reef.

Coral reef cays are relatively young on the Great Barrier Reef, having developed only in the past 6,000 years. Most are unvegetated, still in the early part of their evolution. Sixty-five are established as vegetated cays and 45 are "low wooded" islands - a type of mangrove-colonised cay found only on the reef north of Cairns.

Although the Great Barrier Reef is a World Heritage Listed marine park, it is managed as a "multiple use protected area" - that is, based on ecologically sustainable development principles strictly monitored by both federal and state governments. While commercial mining and oil drilling are prohibited on the Reef, many human activities are permitted under a three-zone system that ranges from a general use zone where most ecologically sustainable pursuits are allowed, to a zone that is hands-off except for scientific research.

Tourism is the giant of commercial activity on the Great Barrier Reef with over two million visitors each year taking advantage of its numerous "tropical paradise" locations. Tourism is permitted in 99.8% of the Marine Park on a permit system and is estimated to return $1.4 billion annually to the Queensland economy. Growing at the rate of 10% per year, Great Barrier Reef tourism in the Nineties has undergone a rapid change from a "slow-boat" style of reef operation to an upmarket, competitive industry that is offering the visitor a wide range of options to choose from. The focus is now on scuba diving, snorkelling, semi-submersible and glass-bottom boat coral viewing. There is a swing towards education and an appreciation of what is, after all, a unique part of the planet.

Fishing in the Great Barrier Reef Marine Park constitutes two separate commercial divisions, trawling and line fishing, which together generate $400 million per year. The effects of both trawling and line fishing on the ecology of the Great Barrier Reef Marine Park, and other concerns such as pollution and vandalism, prompted the Federal and Queensland governments to develop a 25 year Strategic Plan that has become "a perpetual plan for the protection, wise use, understanding and enjoyment of the Great Barrier Reef." More than 60 organisations and key individuals throughout the nation were involved in implementing the Plan which is seen as a co-operative vision by all users of the Marine Park to safeguard its future.

Now, the preservation of the world's largest Marine Park seems assured for all time. The Australian Government's controlling body, the Great Barrier Reef Marine Park Authority, has declared its philosophy and intentions to be: "Our oceans and our entire coastal environment need a new style of management, which recognises that the economic and sustenance factors, the environmental aspect and the rights of human enjoyment be treated fairly in an equitable program known as 'sustainable development'."

Above: Elford Reef.

One of two pontoons located permanently on Moore Reef.

Coral bommies dot the sheltered waters on the lee side of Moore Reef.

Taking a close look at Fairy Basslets and soft coral.

A clown fish seeks refuge within an anemone.

Seeing eye to eye with a potato cod.

Surrounded by Basslets adjacent to a drop off.

Soft corals and sponges make a beautiful underwater garden for both reef dwellers and visiting divers.

A cyclist hurtles around a downhill bend in the Mountain Bike World Cup at Smithfield.

Numerous rapids offer a challenge to whitewater rafters on the Tully River.

Runners from Gordonvale make the punishing 922 metre climb for the annual Pyramid race.

The graceful manoeuvre of a not-too-terrified bungy jumper.

A trusting handler offers a fair reward to Scarsides, a 3 metre male crocodile, after performing at Hartley's Creek.

Young crocodiles display remarkable tolerance when bred in captivity.

Cassowary.

A kangaroo and her joey.

The intense colour of a Ulysses Butterfly.

Goulds Monitor is a large reptile which is commonly referred to as a goanna.

Australia's handsome native dog, the Dingo.

A honeyeater feasts on the flowers of the Umbrella tree.

Koalas are found in small colonies near Herberton on the Atherton Tableland.

Swamp Bloodwood (Eucalyptus Ptychocarpa) in flower.

Enormous raintrees spread their limbs, laden with ribbon ferns, over the highway north of Mossman.

The exquisite flower of the Torch Ginger (Etlinger Elatior).

The Poinciana creates a stunning display just prior to the Wet Season.

Climbing Pandanus in flower.

The early morning tranquility of Marina Mirage, Port Douglas.

Game fishing boats await charter at Port Douglas.

A container ship heads south inside the reef, as fishermen try their early morning luck off the point.

Dawn on the North Johnstone River at Innisfail.

Interesting architecture is a feature of this main street of Innisfail.

A cane train passes through the main street of Mossman.

An idyllic afternoon view from Taylor Point towards Double Island.

Palm Cove is a popular beach destination for holiday makers.

Cane trains are the preferred way to transport sugar cane to the crushing mills.

Steam frames the summit of Walsh's Pyramid in this dawn view of the Gordonvale Sugar Mill.

The afternoon sun highlights flowering sugar cane in suburban Freshwater.

Modern machinery has made the task of harvesting cane much easier.

Locally produced tea is grown in plantations in the cool hills above Innisfail.

Dairy cows are a common sight on the lush rolling hills of the Atherton Tableland.

Pawpaws are one of the many tropical fruits grown in North Queensland.

Sugar cane is the most important and widespread agricultural crop in North Queensland.

The Rainforests

Rainforests have been described as the cradle of evolution, the nursery of the world's incredible richness and diversity of life. In Australia, our own tropical rainforests cover an area of approximately 11,000 square kilometres, stretching from Townsville to Cooktown in a great storehouse of genetic marvels. The Wet Tropics of Queensland are scientific wonders - living museums of rare flora and fauna that represent, with surviving rainforests in New Caledonia and Madagascar, the remaining species of the ancient supercontinent, Gondwanaland. Biological change took place during 35 million years of isolation as the Australian continent drifted north, colliding with the Asian geological plate about 15 million years ago. Then, in a remarkable fusion of species, flora and fauna lifeforms from two entirely different "nurseries" created a virtual time capsule of evolutionary history.

The rainforests of the Australian Wet Tropics are internationally recognised as holding the key to one very important stage of the earth's biological formation - that is, the origin, evolution and dispersal of the primitive flowering plants (Angiosperms). Out of 19 families, 13 occur in the Wet Tropics, and two are found nowhere else in the world. Because this area contains the highest concentration of these families on earth, scientists regard it as a living laboratory containing secrets of the earth's formation. Of nearly 1,200 species of higher plants found in the region, only 70 are regarded as common.

The rainforests of the Wet Tropics also provide a sanctuary for many species of animals regarded as relics of ancient Gondwanaland. These species include insects, birds, marsupials, frogs and reptiles. Certain extraordinary insects found in the Wet Tropics rainforests are unique to a very small area, including some whose nearest relatives are found only in the Andes or the Himalayas.

The Wet Tropics of north Queensland was listed as a World Heritage Area in December 1988, after a time of great controversy and outright hostility between the Commonwealth Government and the Queensland Government of the time - which opposed the listing. Fortunately, greater education on the importance of the rainforests has resulted in a universal acceptance of the legislation among Australians today. As a means of honouring World Heritage criteria, the Wet Tropics Management Authority was established to "protect, conserve, rehabilitate, present, and transmit to future generations" the rainforests of Queensland.

The World Heritage Area is a complex tenure of national parks, state forests, timber reserves, Aboriginal and freehold land as well as many other leases and reserves. More than 300,000 people live in, or near, the World Heritage Area and at least one million tourists visit each year. The Wet Tropics of Queensland is the only tropical rainforest World Heritage Area in a developed country.

That this is an area worth protecting is now beyond question. The region is spectacular in its beauty. Mountain ranges averaging one thousand metres high fall directly into the sea in some areas, with rainforest tumbling to the very beachline. Giant, 3,000 year old trees have survived earlier logging periods and rise majestically out of the rainforest canopy. Dense vine forests, strangler figs and a myriad flora lifeforms compete for light and space in a primaeval struggle for survival. Rugged gorges and waterfalls, including Wallaman Falls, one of the highest in Australia, provide breathtaking vistas rarely equalled elsewhere in the country. The Wet Tropics Management Authority, on behalf of the Australian people, now stands guard over this priceless natural heritage.

The earliest custodians of the rainforests, however, were the Aborigines who have occupied the area continuously for at least 50,000 years. To these indigenous people, the rainforest landscape was a cultural and life-supporting homeland that had always been part of their spiritual Dreamtime.

The original rainforest-dwelling Aborigines were hunter-gatherers who belonged to tribal groups with distinct

Above: Old rainforest giants near The Crater, Mt Hypipamee National Park.

Long, sinewy fingers of a buttressed root fig stretch out across the rainforest floor.

territorial areas, such as the lowland people and others who belonged in the higher rainforests and further back on the Atherton Tableland. An unusual feature of the true rainforest Aborigines was their sophisticated use of toxic plants as food. Using complicated leaching techniques, natural poisons were eliminated from certain rainforest fruits, such as the Black Bean and Yellow Walnut, until they were safe to eat. This constant, everyday use of toxic plant foods distinguished the rainforest people from other Aboriginal cultures in Australia where the practice was only occasional. Tidal fish traps constructed by the Aborigines of Hinchinbrook Island were both complex and effective, utilising stones cemented together by rock oysters forming a natural mortar. Despite the impacts of European settlement, there is a strong continuity of this Aboriginal culture to the present day.

North Queensland's rainforests were always under threat from three main sources - timber exploitation, mining and agriculture. The early timber industry in particular saw the vast forests of hardwoods and cabinet woods as inexhaustable, and, despite limited forms of control by the new Colony of Queensland in the 1860s, the felling of trees by the hardy "timber getters" became rampant. Cedar cutters followed explorer George Dalrymple's 1873 expedition along the north-east Queensland coast, crossing the Daintree River into the heartland of what is today the Wet Tropics region. Cutters claimed a prize tree simply by felling it, even if it was in an inaccessible location, simply to prevent their rivals claiming it. William Pettigrew, pioneer Queensland sawmiller, wrote: "As a rule timber cutters all hate one another (and) the amount of timber however wasted is enormous."

Prime cedar logs were rafted to river mouths, loaded on to ships and transported to the southern colonies. Queensland received no revenue from the southern timber barons and the plunder of the rainforests continued until, by the end of the 1870s, the Mossman and Daintree valleys were almost completely cut out. Then, with the discovery of tin on the Atherton Tableland, timber cutters rushed to exploit the new "cedar fields" and in 1881 cedar had become a common building material. Millions of superfeet were lost as logs floating down the Barron River were hopelessly snagged, smashed to splinters over the Barron Falls at Kuranda, or washed out to sea. As with the coastal rainforests, timber lay on the ground where it was felled, until finally the Land Commissioner refused to issue more licenses.

The world's remaining rainforests are being destroyed at the alarming rate of over 12 million hectares per year. In addition, continuing activities such as hunting, fuelwood gathering, mining, logging and agriculture are degrading even larger tracts of virgin forest. A United Nations report in 1981 assessed that only 12 million square kilometres of tropical rainforest remained on the planet. More than a decade later, this figure would have reduced dramatically. Australia's protective legislation of the Wet Tropics rainforests has set an example for other countries and ensures that these ancient forests remain undisturbed to continue their evolutionary growth into the future.

Above: Low cloud sweeps over forest clad mountains.

Wonderful circular shapes form the canopy of a fan palm forest of Licuala Ramsayii.

An enormous strangler fig dominates this section of forest near Cedar Bay.

MAJOR PARKS OF NORTH QUEENSLAND

North Queensland national parks cover a large, diverse area of Crown land including tropical islands and reefs, rain-forested mountains, coastal wetlands, fossil fields, Aboriginal rock art galleries and a wide expanse of rugged outback country. Some of these parks fall within the Wet Tropics World Heritage Area - a region of about 900,000 hectares.

The parks are managed by the Queensland National Parks and Wildlife Service which is responsible for the overall conservation and protection of all flora and fauna within the parks. Animals in national parks are protected by the *Fauna Conservation Act*, whereby all native mammals, birds and terrestrial reptiles are Crown property. Rare and endangered species are totally protected in the wild from human interference. Camping facilities and walking tracks in most national parks encourage human activity and are becoming increasingly popular with overseas visitors.

Cape York Peninsula national parks, in particular, are outstanding in their natural beauty. Open woodlands and plains provide stark contrasts to the richly vegetated mountains, rivers and waterfalls of the coast. Dominating the Cape are four major river systems - the Jardine, Archer, Mitchell and Normanby - all flowing west and north from the Great Dividing Range. By contrast, the smaller - though wildly spectacular - Daintree River flows eastwards into the Great Barrier Reef.

The Daintree National Park is just 80 kilometres north of Cairns and an important part of the Wet Tropics World Heritage Area. The 56,500 hectare park is largely inaccessible, rising from the Daintree and Mossman rivers into the high rainfall slopes of the Mount Carbine Tablelands. In its tumbling 20 kilometre journey to the sea, the Mossman River has carved a steep-sided gorge through granite and rainforest. The park comprises several different types of forest, from the tall-canopied lowland forest to the drier, open bush on the western slopes and the stunted, wind-swept vegetation on the mountain tops. The beautiful blue Ulysses and the green and black Cairns Birdwing butterflies dance along the edges of Mossman Gorge, a popular freshwater swimming and picnic area. The swirling, cold currents of the river are refreshing in winter, but can be dangerous during the wet summer season when torrential rain floods the waterways of the area.

A profusion of plant life competes for light and space in the dense rainforest of this national park. Large and small tree trunks literally "reach for the sky", their leafy crowns forming a blanket canopy that blocks out all but the occasional ray of sunlight from the forest floor. Ferns and orchids have adapted to life in the canopy, while on the ground decaying trees support mosses, fungi and a host of other plants suited to the humid conditions.

Rarely seen marsupials, such as the tree-climbing kangaroo and musky rat-kangaroo take advantage of the safe haven provided by the park, and a wide variety of exotic birds feed and play in the treetops.

Further north, the Cape Tribulation National Park covers an area between the Daintree and Bloomfield rivers. Named by Captain James Cook in 1770 after his ship "Endeavour" was holed on a nearby reef, the area is a constant reminder of the great mariner's misfortune on his journey north along Queensland's coastline. Backed by the McDowall Range as its western boundary, the 16,959 hectare park slopes steeply up from the coast to the mountains.

Regarded as one of the most spectacular national parks in the world, Cape Tribulation enjoys the distinction of being part of one World Heritage Area and bordering another - the Great Barrier Reef Marine Park. The park is a rich mosaic of diverse ecosystems which include coastal mangroves, swamps, lowland and upland rainforests and mountaintop heathlands.

The Daintree region continues to astound scientists by

Above: Thornton Peak, Cape Tribulation National Park.

Rainforest spills down to the beach at Cape Tribulation.

The Bouncing Stones of Thornton Beach, Cape Tribulation National Park.

revealing new species of flora and fauna - living up to its international reputation as a "living laboratory" and "evolutionary cradle" of the earth's pre-history. Among the strange and colourful wildlife found in the rainforests, the cassowary stands out as a prime example of the park's unique fauna. This giant flightless bird grows to a height of two metres and is fiercely protective of its territory. Equipped with a tough, cartilage helmet or "casque", normally used for "ploughing" through thick undergrowth, it can also be used aggressively against intruders - including humans! The cassowary should be observed at a safe distance and its territory respected.

Estuarine, or "saltwater" crocodiles inhabit the Daintree National Park and are of course extremely dangerous. These fascinating creatures have remained unchanged for 200 million years, having lived alongside the great dinosaurs and survived the breakup of ancient continents and at least two million years of periodic Ice Ages. Crocodiles are threatened with extinction, especially in south-east Asia, but in Australia they are protected by law.

In recent years, Cape Tribulation - or "Trib", as it is commonly known - has become a mecca for tourists, especially backpacker travellers. The isolation and beauty of the region has made it famous worldwide and its popularity has caused debate among conservationists who fear an overload of human traffic will destroy the natural quality of the environment.

The beaches, reefs and coastal waters bordering the Cape Tribulation National Park are protected and fishing, spearfishing and collecting are prohibited between Cape Tribulation and Bloomfield. Limited fishing is allowed in other areas. Raised boardwalks through mangrove thickets and coastal waterways lead to platforms overlooking panoramic beach and ocean views.

Bellenden Ker National Park is a magnificent mountain wilderness surrounding Mt Bartle Frere, Queensland's highest peak. Towering 1622 metres above the coastal lowlands, the summit offers unparalleled ocean views to the east and views of the Atherton Tableland to the west. Mt Bellenden Ker itself, at 1593 metres, falls just short of its higher neighbour. This region is Australia's wettest, with annual rainfalls exceeding 10 metres quite common.

As a result, rivers, streams and waterfalls cascade through lush rainforests into the ocean below. Due to the dramatic changes in altitude, the mountain is clothed in different types of rainforest. From tall, large-leafed forest on the foothills, the vegetation changes to a smaller-leaf, lower canopy, on to a low, wind-swept type above 1500 metres. The summit is a wild, boulder-strewn environment that can cloud over without warning. Sudden rainstorms are also common and temperatures can drop rapidly at night throughout the year.

Despite the rugged terrain, bushwalkers regularly make the climb to the top of Mt Bartle Frere. Starting at Josephine Falls, a well-known swimming spot about 50 kilometres south of Cairns, the climb is a tough 7.5 kilometre haul which should only be attempted by fit, well-equipped bushwalkers. The track is clearly marked, but undeveloped, and inexperienced walkers have become lost on the climb. The return trip takes a minimum of 12 hours, but the Queensland National Parks and Wildlife Service advises camping overnight on the slopes.

Walking tracks are a feature of the Bellenden Ker National Park. In the Palmerston Section of the park, along the Palmerston Highway from Innisfail to the Atherton Tableland, tracks vary in length from 800 metres at Henrietta Creek to the 7.2 kilometre Nandroya Falls circuit walk.

Named after explorer Christie Palmerston, who blazed a trail over the mountains in 1882, the highway cuts through some of the finest World Heritage rainforest in North Queensland. More than 500 species of trees survive in this environment, once the home and spiritual "Dreaming" place of five Aboriginal tribes.

One of North Queensland's most popular walking tracks traverses Bellenden Ker National Park. From its starting point at Babinda Boulders Scenic Reserve, the Goldfield Trail crosses 19 kilometres of creeks, ridges, valleys and old logging tracks to its final destination in the Goldsborough Valley State Forest camping area. The trail was first hacked out of the wilderness in the 1930s by William Kraft after he discovered gold on the north-western slopes of Mt Bartle Frere. When the gold petered out the trail was abandoned until 1986, when members of the international volunteer organisation, Operation Raleigh, reopened it. Now, hikers regularly use the trail, which can usually be completed in 7-9 hours.

Bellenden Ker National Park encompasses 79,500 hectares of wild mountain terrain, making it the largest rainforest park in Queensland and an outstanding feature of the Wet Tropics World Heritage Area.

Lake Barrine, on the Atherton Tableland, is a crater lake formed by two massive underground explosions resulting in a water catchment 65 metres deep. Completely surrounded by rainforest, Lake Barrine - and its close neighbour, Lake Eacham, just three kilometres away - is a geological remnant of intense volcanic activity that continued on the Tableland until 100,000 years ago.

At the beginning of a 6.5 kilometre walking track near the water's edge, two giant Kauri pine trees stand side by side like sentinels guarding the ancient secrets of the lake. The trees are descendants of a species that dominated Tableland forests for thousands of years. These Kauris are almost identical to fossil Kauris found in rocks 300 million years old.

Above: Nandroya Falls, Palmerston National Park.

Lowland sugar and rainforest are dominated by The Bluff, which overlooks Mossman Gorge, Daintree National Park.

Surrounded by mountains and rainforest, the cool clear waters of Mossman Gorge attract many day visitors.

Countless massive granite boulders form the highly unusual Black Mountain near Cooktown.

The smoothly sculpted granite rocks of the Boulders, near Babinda, are worn smooth by waters from Mount Bartle Frere.

Torrents of water pour through the lower section of the falls, Barron Falls National Park.

The world renowned Tjapukai Dance Theatre is based in Kuranda.

Human or spirit figures and a crocodile, painted several thousand years ago at Brady Creek, Jowalbinna, near Laura.

An old lady figure or widow adorned with a magical pendant beside two dingoes, Jowalbinna, near Laura.

Unlike the friendly quinkans, the knob-tailed spirit figure has a spiteful nature. Split Rock near Laura.

The Undara Lava Tubes are some of the world's best examples of volcanic flow.

The limestone caves near Chillagoe.

Pellowe Reef.

First published by Thunderhead Publishing 1995
First reprint 1995
Second reprint 1996
PO Box 549 Kuranda Qld 4872 Australia
Telephone (070) 93 7171 Facsimile (070) 93 8897

Photography by Peter Jarver, Master of Photography, AIPP
Text written by Robert Reid
Original design by Adrian Schoots
Concept and photographic layout by Peter Jarver
Printed in Hong Kong by South China Printing Co.
© Peter Jarver 1995

Jarver, Peter
Cairns, Reef to Rainforest
ISBN 0 9589067 3 4

All rights reserved. No part of this publication may be reproduced, stored in a retrieval system or transmitted in any form or by any means, electronic, mechanical, photocopying, recording or otherwise, without prior permission of the publisher.

ACKNOWLEDGEMENTS

Nick Tonks for photographs on pages 32 and 33
Marilyn Venus for editing assistance
Tjapukai Dance Theatre for photograph on page 60
Hartley's Creek Crocodile Farm
Wild World
Paul Wright of the Australian Butterfly Sanctuary
Peter Shanahan of the Flecker Botanical Gardens
Department of Environment and Heritage
Paul and Jeanette Lewis
Mathew Trezise of Trezise Bush Guides
Rob Fullerton of Undara Lava Lodge
Cairns Port Authority
Great Adventures

Green Island